PRE-SCHOOL LOWERCASE ALPHABET

Fun-filled Activities

An imprint of Om Books International

The Letter a

Read the name of each picture aloud. Write **a** for the pictures names of which begin with the letter **a**.

Trace and write a.

a a a

The Letter b

Read the name of each picture aloud. Circle (O) all the pictures names of which begin with the letter **b**.

Trace and write b.

b b b

The Letter c

Read aloud the name of each picture. Tick (✓) all the pictures names of which begin with the letter **c**.

Trace and write c.

c c c

The Letter d

Read aloud the name of each picture. Write **d** for the pictures names of which begin with the letter **d**.

d

dog

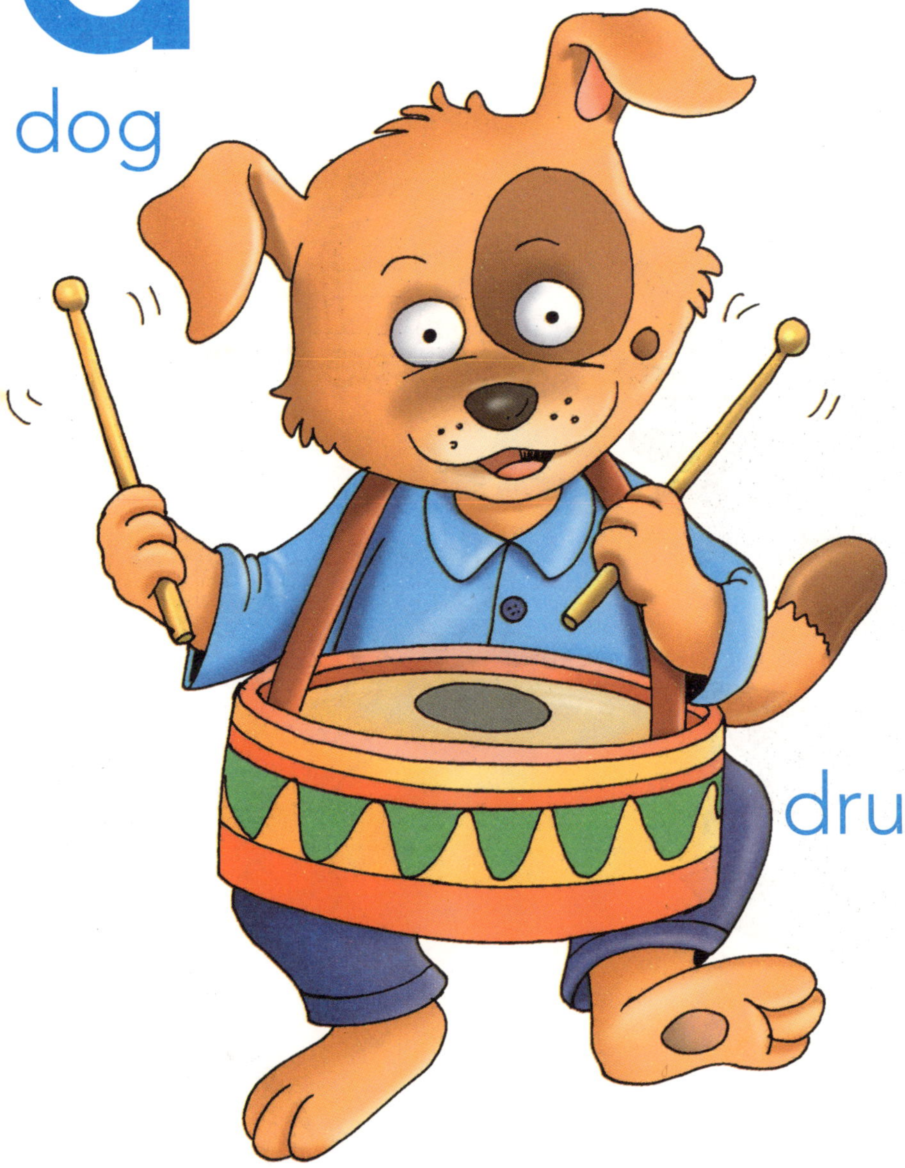

drum

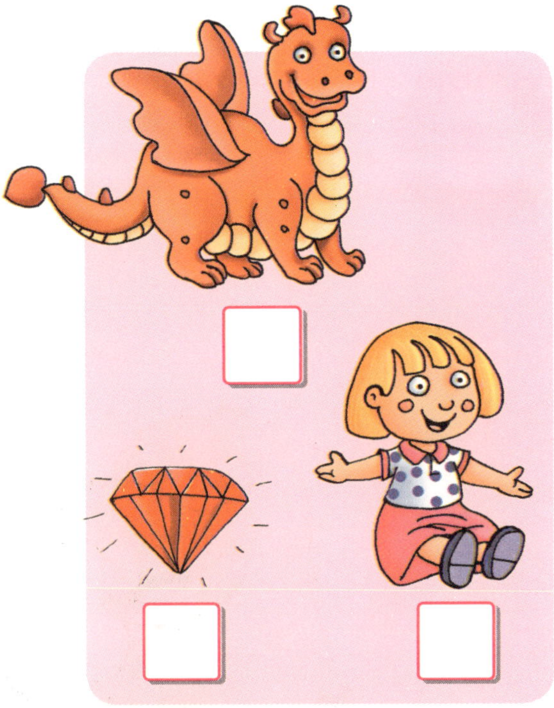

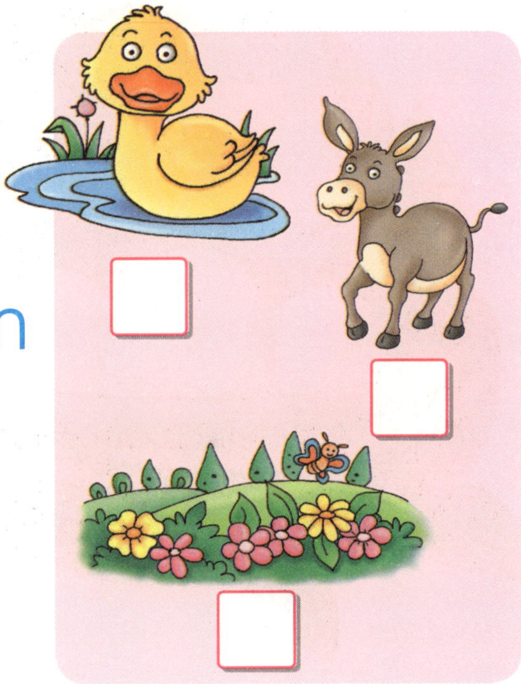

Trace and write d.

The Letter e

Read aloud the name of each picture. Circle (O) all the pictures names of which begin with the letter **e**.

e

eagle

eggs

Trace and write e.

The Letter f

Read aloud the name of each picture. Tick (✓) all the pictures names of which begin with the letter **f**.

Trace and write f.

f

The Letter g

Read aloud the name of each picture. Write **g** for the pictures names of which begin with the letter **g**.

goat

grass

Trace and write g.

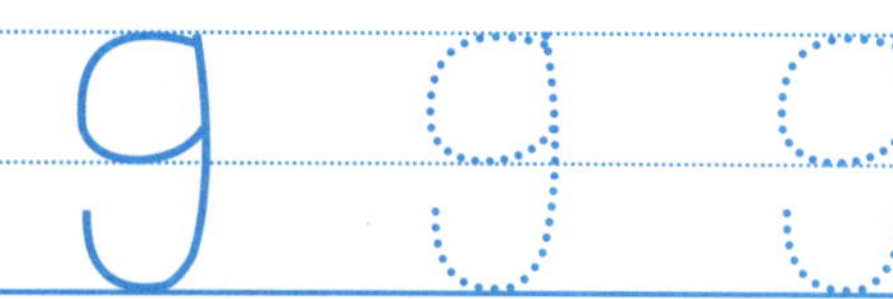

The Letter h

Read aloud the name of each picture. Circle (O) all the pictures names of which begin with the letter **h**.

Trace and write h.

The Letter i

Read aloud the name of each picture. Tick (✓) all the pictures names of which begin with the letter i.

Trace and write i.

Fun With Letters

Tick (✓) the pictures the names of which begin with the given letters.

The Letter j

Read aloud the name of each picture. Write j for the pictures names of which begin with the letter j.

Trace and write j.

j j j

The Letter k

Read aloud the name of each picture. Circle (O) all the pictures names of which begin with the letter **k**.

Trace and write k.

k k k

The Letter l

Read aloud the name of each picture. Tick (✓) all the pictures names of which begin with the letter l.

Trace and write l.

The Letter m

Read aloud the name of each picture. Write **m** for the pictures names of which begin with the letter **m**.

moon

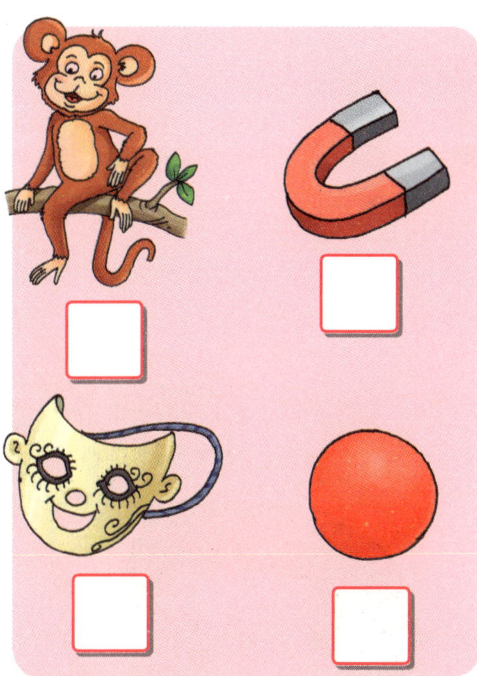

mouse

Trace and write m.

The letter N

Read aloud the name of each picture. Circle (O) all the pictures names of which begin with the letter **n**.

Trace and write n.

n n n

The Letter o

Read aloud the name of each picture. Tick (✓) all the pictures names of which begin with the letter o.

Trace and write o.

The Letter p

Read aloud the name of each picture. Write **p** for the pictures names of which begin with the letter **p**.

Trace and write p.

p p p

The Letter q

Read aloud the name of each picture. Circle (O) all the pictures names of which begin with the letter **q**.

Trace and write q.

The Letter r

Read aloud the name of each picture. Tick (✓) all the pictures names of which begin with the letter **r**.

Trace and write r.

r r r

The Letter s

Read aloud the name of each picture. Write **s** for the pictures names of which begin with the letter **s**.

sun

snail

Trace and write s.

The Letter t

Read aloud the name of each picture. Circle (O) all the pictures names of which begin with the letter **t**.

Trace and write t.

t t t

The Letter u

Read aloud the name of each picture. Tick (✓) all the pictures names of which begin with the letter **u**.

Trace and write u.

u u u

The Letter v

Read aloud the name of each picture. Write **v** for the pictures names of which begin with the letter **v**.

Trace and write v.

v v v

The Letter w

Read aloud the name of each picture. Circle (O) all the pictures names of which begin with the letter **w**.

Trace and write w.

w w w

The Letter x

Read aloud the name of each picture. Tick (✓) all the pictures names of which begin with the letter **x**.

Trace and write x.

x x x

The Letter y

Read aloud the name of each picture. Write **y** for the pictures names of which begin with the letter **y**.

Trace and write y.

y y y

The Letter z

Read aloud the name of each picture. Circle (O) all the pictures names of which begin with the letter **z**.

Trace and write z.

z z z

Fun With Letters

Write the beginning letter of the name of each picture.

Draw a line through the pictures that start with the same letter.

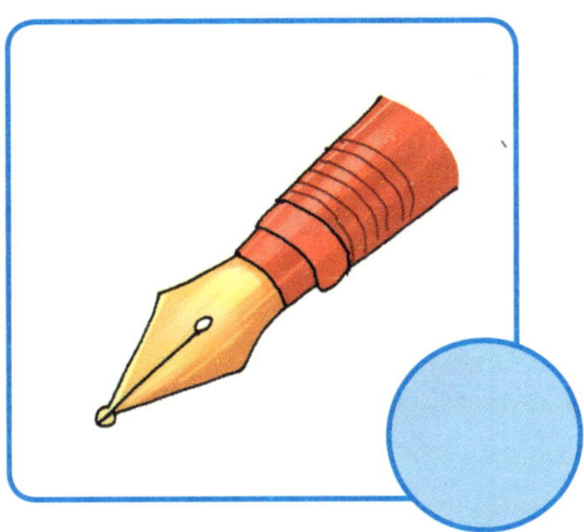

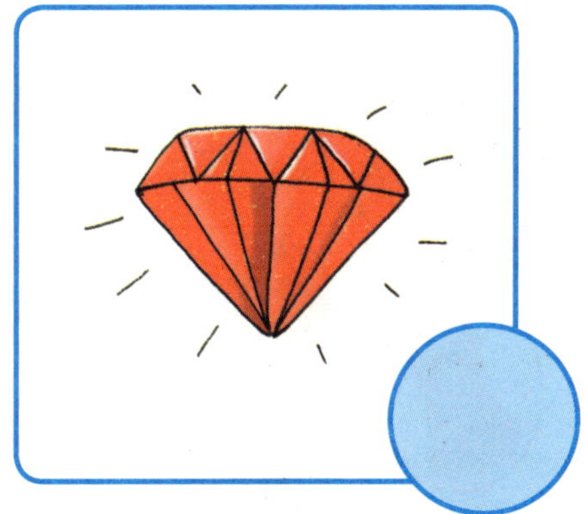

Answer Key

Page 2

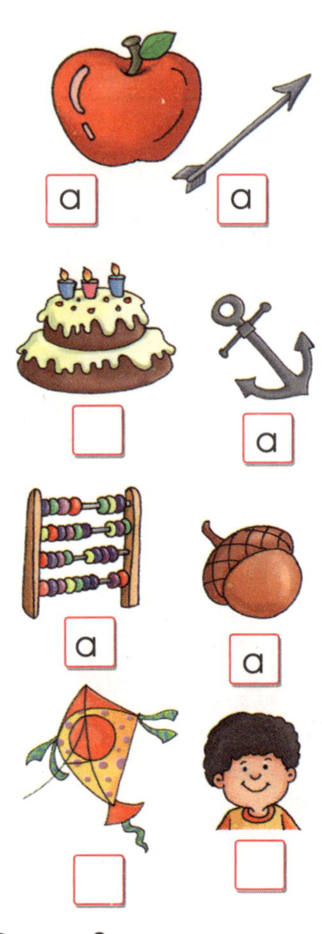

Page 3

Page 4

Page 5

Page 6

Page 7

Page 8

Page 9

Answer Key

Page 10

Page 11

Page 12

Page 13

Page 14

Page 15

Page 16

Page 17

Answer Key

Page 19

Page 20

Page 21

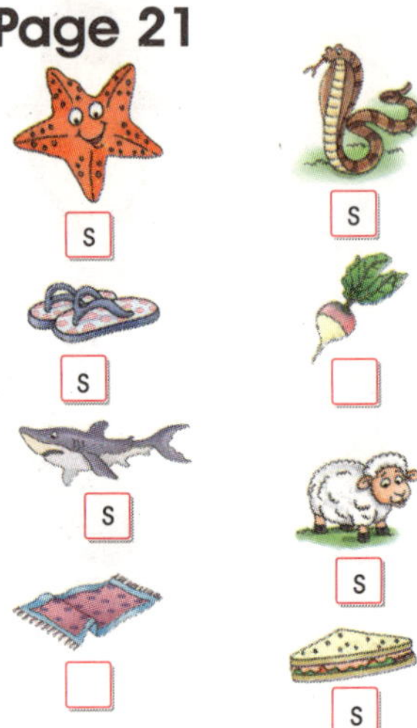

Page 22

Page 23

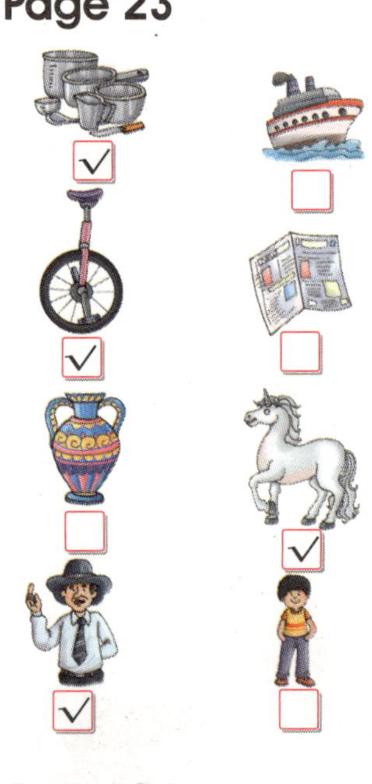

Page 24

Page 25

Page 26

Page 27

Page 28

Page 29